HOW TO DRAW
CHRISTMAS

Mark Bergin

Hatch

First published in the UK in 2018 by The Salariya Book Company Ltd
This edition published in the UK in 2024 by Hatch Press,
an imprint of Bonnier Books UK
4th Floor, Victoria House
Bloomsbury Square, London WC1B 4DA
Owned by Bonnier Books
Sveavägen 56, Stockholm, Sweden
www.bonnierbooks.co.uk

Copyright © 2024 by Hatch Press

1 3 5 7 9 10 8 6 4 2

All rights reserved

ISBN 978-1-83587-002-0

Printed in China

Contents

- 4 .... Making a start
- 6 .... Drawing materials
- 8 .... Perspective
- 10 .... Using photos
- 12 .... Robin
- 14 .... Snowman
- 16 .... Decorations
- 18 .... Holly
- 20 .... Christmas alphabet
- 22 .... Christmas wreath
- 24 .... Christmas tree
- 26 .... Santa Claus
- 28 .... Santa Claus' sleigh
- 30 .... Nativity scene
- 32 .... Glossary and Index

Making a start

Learning to draw is about looking and seeing. Keep practising and get to know your subject. Use a sketchbook to make quick drawings. Start by doodling, and experiment with shapes and patterns. There are many ways to draw, and this book shows only some of them. Look at Christmas cards, shop window displays, illustrators' drawings and see how friends draw, but above all, find your own way.

Candle

Stocking

Snowmen

Presents

Practise drawing from physical objects or photographs. Build up your drawings using simple shapes.

Drawing materials

Try using different types of drawing paper and materials. Experiment with charcoal, wax crayons and pastels. All pens, from felt-tips to ballpoints, will make interesting marks – or try drawing with pen and ink on wet paper.

Ink silhouette

Pencil drawings can include a vast amount of detail and tone. Try experimenting with different grades of pencil to get a range of light and shade effects in your drawing.

Pencil

Remember, the best equipment and materials will not necessarily make the best drawing - only practice will!

Lines drawn in **ink** cannot be erased, so keep your ink drawings sketchy and less rigid. Don't worry about mistakes, as these lines can be lost in the drawing as it develops.

Adding light and shade to a drawing with an ink pen can be tricky. Use solid ink for the very darkest areas and cross-hatching for ordinary dark tones. Use hatching for midtones, and leave the white of the paper for the lightest areas.

Crosshatching is the use of straight lines that criss-cross each other.
Hatching is when short parallel lines are used to create tone.

Ink

Felt-tip pen

Felt-tips come in a range of line widths. The wider pens are good for filling in large areas of flat tone.

Perspective

If you look at anything from different viewpoints, you will see that the part that is closest to you looks larger, and the part furthest away from you looks smaller. Drawing in perspective is a way of creating a feeling of space - of showing three dimensions on a flat surface.

The vanishing point (V.P.) is the place in a perspective drawing where parallel lines appear to meet. The position of the vanishing point depends on the viewer's eye level.

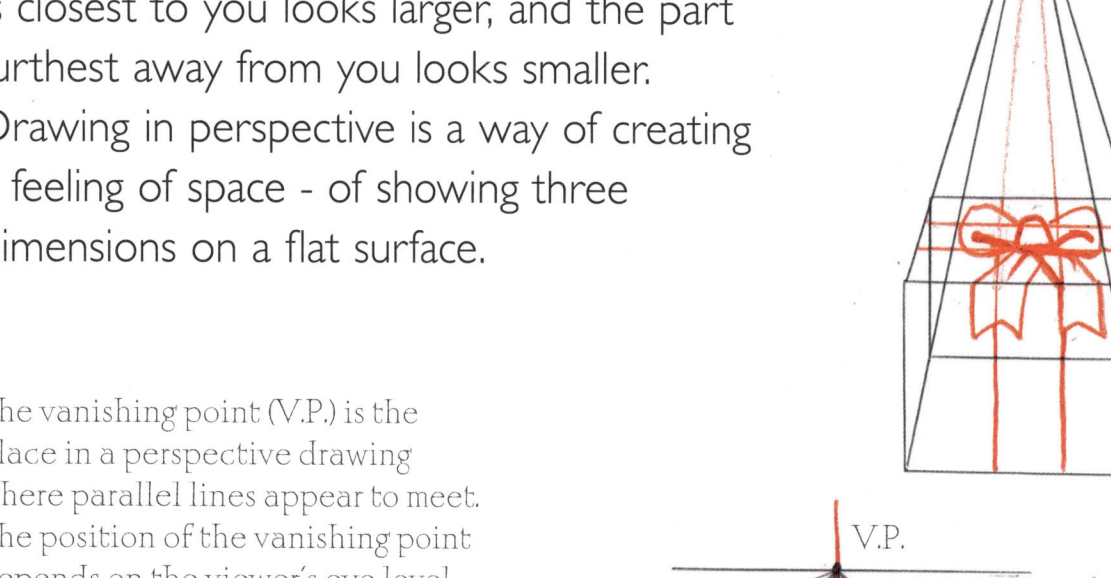

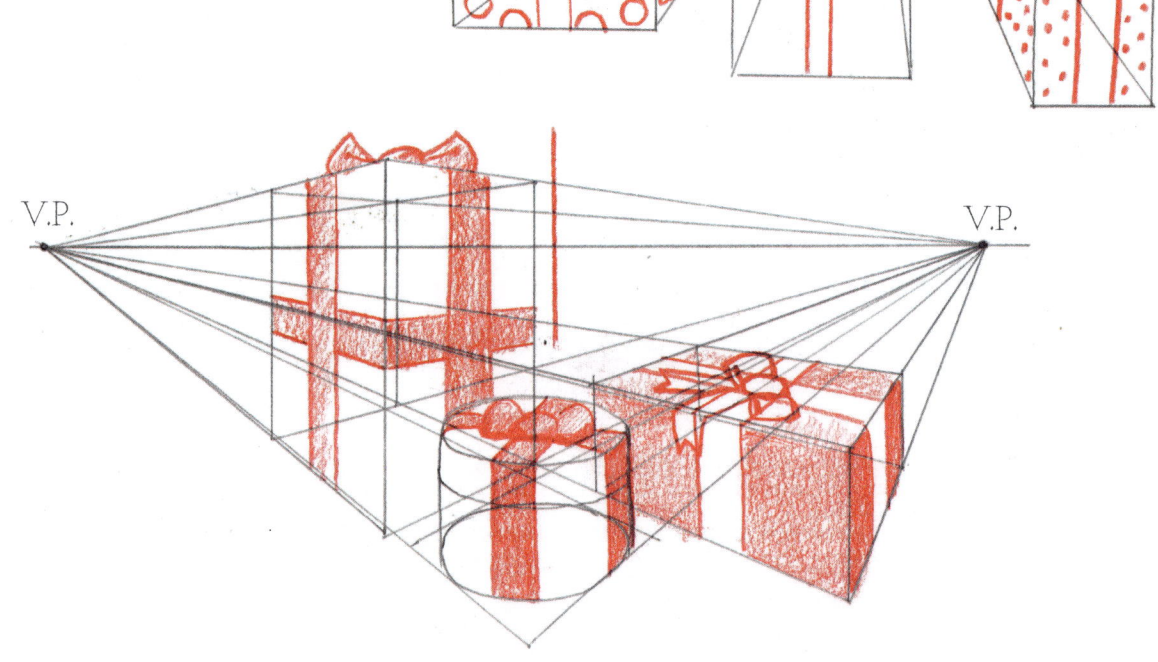

Two-point perspective uses two vanishing points: one for lines running along the length of the subject, and one on the opposite side for lines running across the width of the subject.

Using photos

Drawing from photographs is a useful way to study shape and proportion. Copying a photograph can be quite instructive and it's much easier than trying to draw a robin (or sleigh...) before it flies off.

Photograph

First choose a good image and trace it. Then draw a grid of squares over the tracing.

Now draw a faint grid of the same proportions onto your drawing paper. To adapt to the size of your drawing paper, simply enlarge or decrease the scale of the grid. Copy the shapes within each square of the tracing paper grid onto your drawing-paper grid.

Decide on a light source for your drawing.

Once the outline shape is complete, add more details to the drawing. Always refer back to the grid for accuracy. To add form to your drawing, see where the light falls, and add shadows to those parts that face away from the light source.

Robin

These red-breasted birds are a species of thrush. They live mainly on insects, and build their nests in walls or trees using moss and leaves. Since the mid-19th century, they have become closely associated with Christmas, featuring on many festive cards and postage stamps.

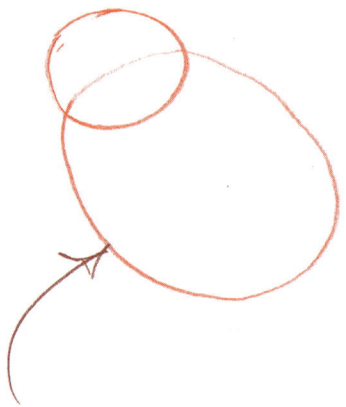

Start by drawing in a circle and an oval for the robin's head and body.

Join the head to the body with curved lines. Draw in the shape of the robin's tail feathers.

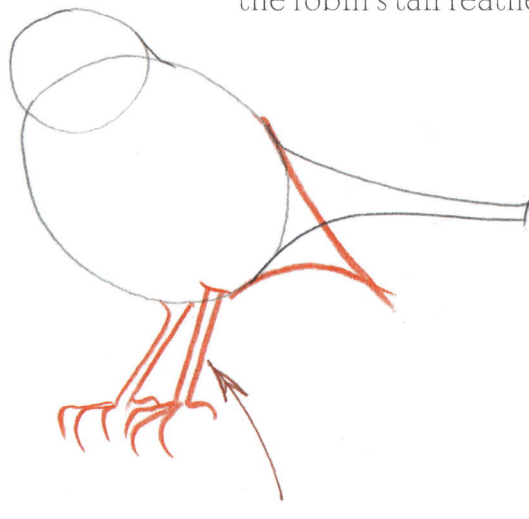

Sketch in the basic shape of the wing feathers and the robin's legs and feet.

Composition

Composition is the arrangement of a picture, or the various parts of a picture, on paper. Does your drawing look better in an upright (portrait) format or as a horizontal (landscape) format?

Draw in the robin's beak and one shiny black eye. Don't forget to leave a highlight! Indicate the robin's red breast area.

Sketch in the tree stump it's perched on and add a sprig of holly, too. Add more detail to the wing formation.

Add shading to create texture and depth of colour to the robin's plumage, and to emphasise the dark berries. Shade in the robin's underbelly and any areas where light doesn't reach.

13

Snowman

Whenever there's a heavy snowfall, the first thing people do is rush outside and make a snowman. The tallest snowman on record was made in Bethel, Maine in the USA in 2008. It stood 122 feet tall!

Start by drawing in two circles, one slightly smaller than the other, for the snowman's head and chest.

Draw a big oval for the bottom half of the snowman. Add construction lines for its arms and broom and a base line.

Now draw in the twig shapes for the snowman's arms and fingers. Draw the broom handle and its head.

Draw in the snowman's face: its eyes, mouth and carrot nose. Add a scarf and buttons.

Draw a robin on the snowman's hat as a finishing touch.

Sketch in the snowman's hat and add shape and tassles to his scarf. Draw in the broom head.

Add a sprig of holly and some more detail to the snowman's battered hat. Add shading to indicate the direction of the light and to create a strong shadow on the snow.

Decorations

Traditional Christmas decorations include bells, boughs of holly, baubles, candy canes, tinsel and mistletoe. This tradition of decorating the home during the festive period dates back at least as far as the 15th century, when fir tree branches and candles were placed indoors.

Start by drawing three circles for the baubles.

Draw in the ring fixtures at the top of each bauble and the ellipses at either end. Add construction lines for the Christmas tree branch.

Start building up more detail: add star and snowflake patterns to the baubles, and include hanging rings. Draw in the shape of the fir tree branch.

Add all finishing touches to the bauble designs. Use short one-directional lines to create the individual needles of the Christmas tree branch. Add shading to create the round form of each bauble.

Holly

There are around 400 species of holly, including English and American varieties which are often used as Christmas decorations. English holly trees have green, spiny leaves and red berries, and can grow up to nearly 50 feet tall.

Start by drawing four construction lines to position the leaves.

Draw in spiky outlines for the two outermost leaves.

Add the other two leaves and draw in the stem.

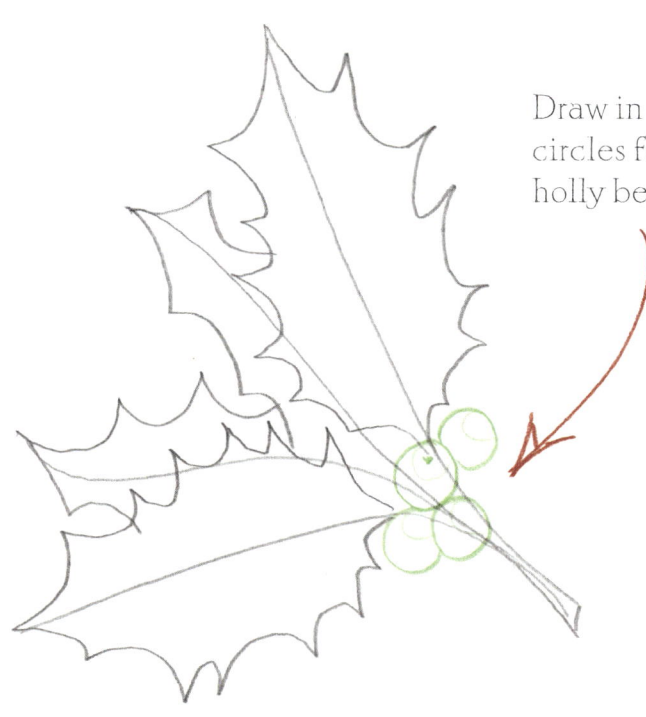

Draw in small circles for the holly berries.

Negative space

Look at the negative space around your drawing, too. This can alert you to any problem areas in the drawing.

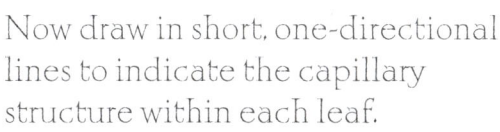

Now draw in short, one-directional lines to indicate the capillary structure within each leaf.

Colour in the berries, leaving white highlights in each. Vary the tone to create their round shape. Add colour to the leaves, but don't forget your light source.

Christmas alphabet

It is fun to create your own hand-drawn lettering. Here is an example of how to design a jolly Christmas-themed alphabet. Use it for cards, invitations and posters, or use it to spell out someone's name to personalise special gifts.

Use construction lines to accurately proportion each letter in your alphabet.

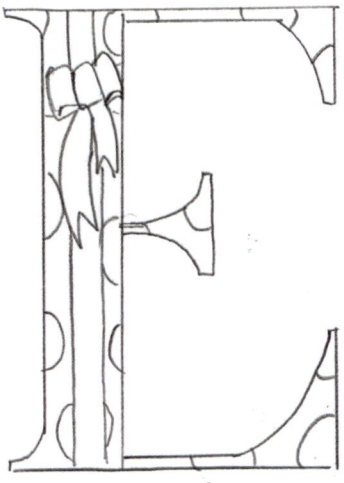

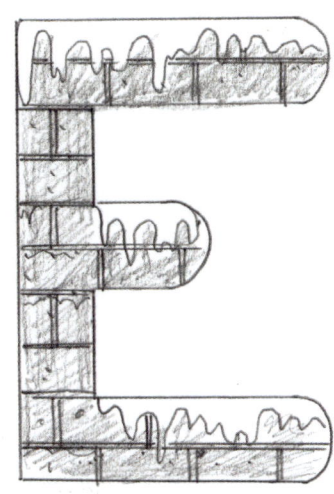

You can create a wide variety of different Christmas themes, such as a gift-wrapped letter or a snow-capped brick letter, as shown in these two examples of the letter 'E'.

Here are some ideas for a Christmas-themed alphabet:

Christmas wreath

Decorative wreaths are displayed at Christmas in the United States, Canada and northern Europe. They usually feature holly leaves and berries. The tradition of using wreaths on religious and festive occasions stretches back at least as far as ancient Egypt, although this practice was later revived during the Italian Renaissance and in Victorian England.

Start by drawing two concentric circles.

Add a bow at the top and curving lines that form the first part of the wreath's decorations.

Now draw in a variety of decorations, including stars, pine cones, bells and berries. Add as many different decorations as you like - be imaginative!

Use lots of small, spiky lines to convey the bristly texture of the foliage. Add shading to darken the foliage and don't forget to leave a glint of the light on each of the decorations.

Christmas tree

Pine and fir are popular choices for Christmas trees, or some people may prefer an artificial one. They are decorated with baubles, lights, a star or an angel figurine on top, and sometimes sweets. The Christmas tree tradition comes from Germany. A fir tree hung with apples was used in medieval plays to represent the Garden of Eden. Families took to setting up similar trees in their homes.

Start by drawing a triangular outline for the tree and the outline of its trunk.

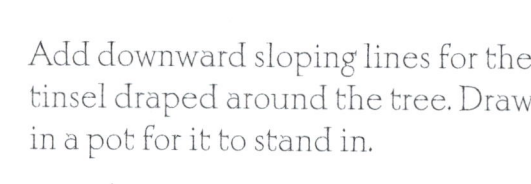

Add downward sloping lines for the tinsel draped around the tree. Draw in a pot for it to stand in.

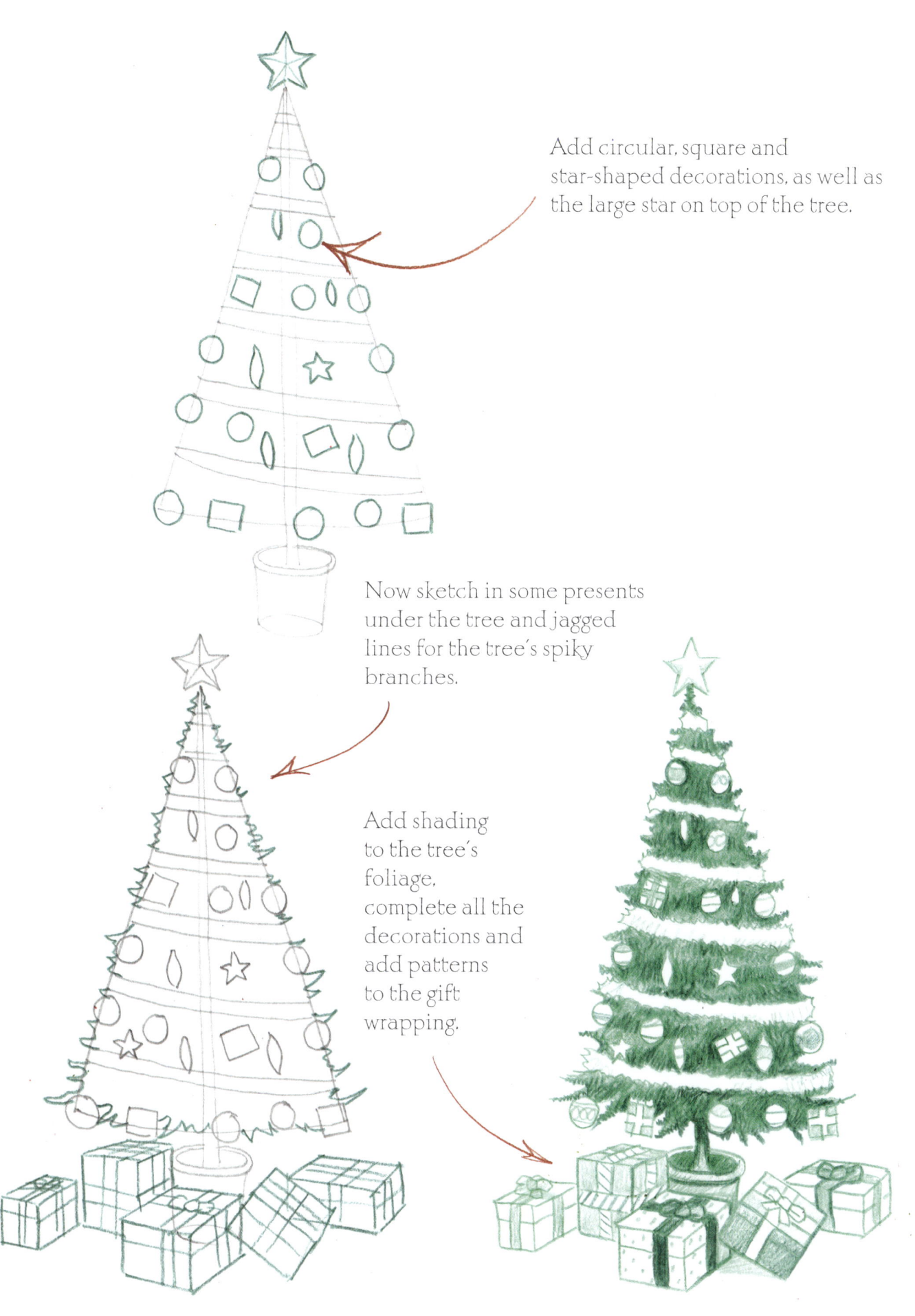

Add circular, square and star-shaped decorations, as well as the large star on top of the tree.

Now sketch in some presents under the tree and jagged lines for the tree's spiky branches.

Add shading to the tree's foliage, complete all the decorations and add patterns to the gift wrapping.

Santa Claus

It is believed that early Dutch emigrants to New York transported the legend of Saint Nicholas, so popularising the tradition of giving gifts to children on his feast day. The Dutch St Nicholas is "Sinter Klaas". The modern image of Santa Claus originates from the images for *Harper's Weekly* by cartoonist Thomas Nast in 1863.

Start by drawing a circle for Santa's head and two ovals for his body. Add a construction line for his spine.

Add lines for Santa's legs with dots at the joints. Draw simple shapes for his feet.

Draw in more lines for his arms with dots for joints. Add simple shapes for his hands and fingers.

Add lines to position his facial features.

Sketch in the sack on his shoulder and his hat. Add his facial features, beard and fingers.

Draw his belt buckle and buttons.

Draw the fur trim and add heels to his boots.

Draw in the shapes of his thick, fur-lined jacket and trousers.

Add toys to his sack for the finishing touch! Finish all detail, and use shading to convey his dark-coloured suit and any areas in shadow.

Use A Mirror

Try looking at your drawing in a mirror. Seeing it in reverse can help you to spot mistakes.

27

Santa Claus' sleigh

The modern idea of Santa's sleigh and the names of his reindeer, comes from the poem *The Night Before Christmas*. It was originally published anonymously in 1823 in the *New York Sentinel*. Rudolph was not invented until 1939, when he featured in a booklet that was sold at Montgomery Ward department stores.

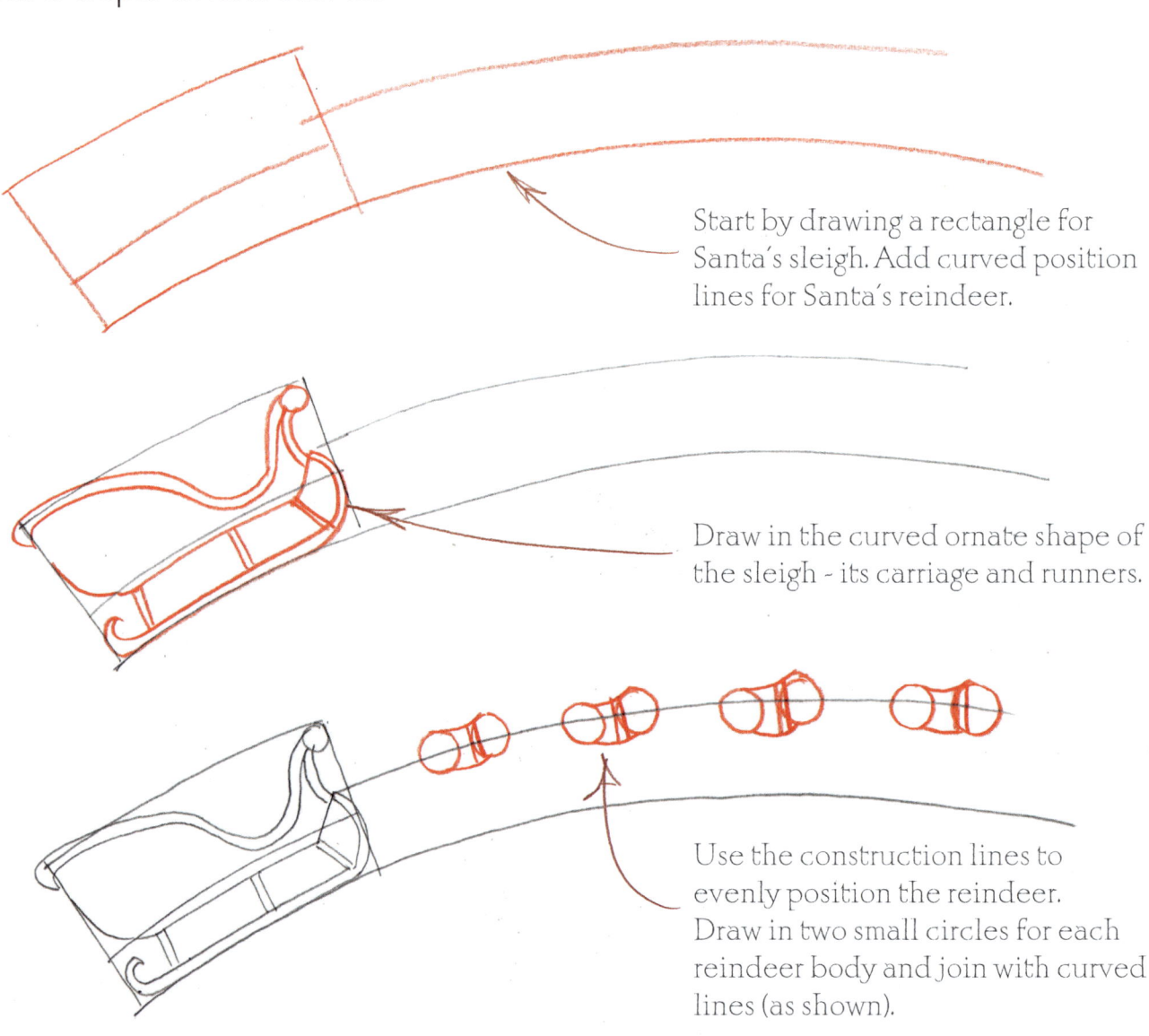

Start by drawing a rectangle for Santa's sleigh. Add curved position lines for Santa's reindeer.

Draw in the curved ornate shape of the sleigh - its carriage and runners.

Use the construction lines to evenly position the reindeer. Draw in two small circles for each reindeer body and join with curved lines (as shown).

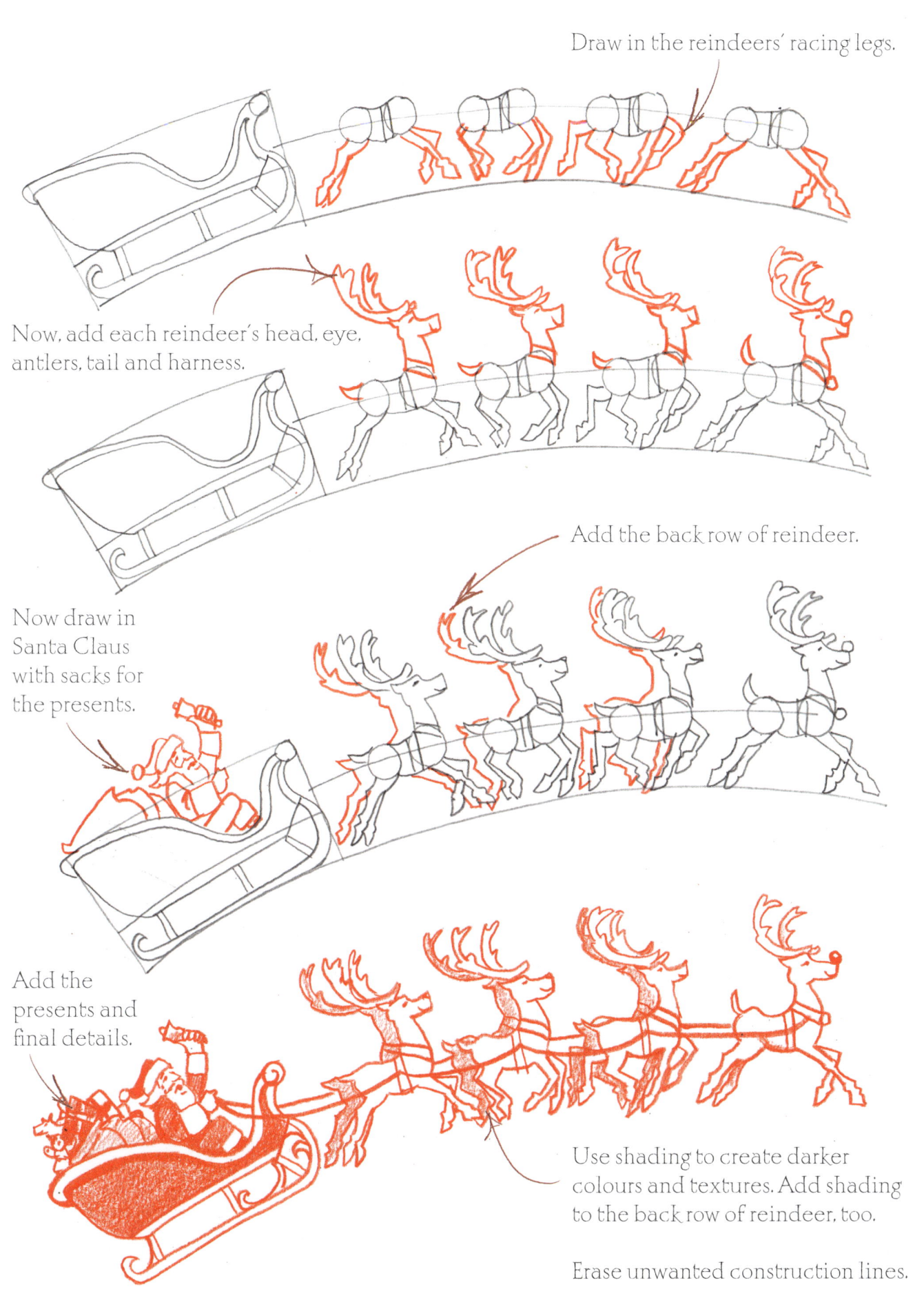

Draw in the reindeers' racing legs.

Now, add each reindeer's head, eye, antlers, tail and harness.

Add the back row of reindeer.

Now draw in Santa Claus with sacks for the presents.

Add the presents and final details.

Use shading to create darker colours and textures. Add shading to the back row of reindeer, too.

Erase unwanted construction lines.

Nativity scene

Inspired by the biblical descriptions of Christ's birth, the Nativity is a popular theme in Christian art. Pictures and models of the scene usually show the baby Jesus, Mary, Joseph and three wise men in the stable where the child was born.

Start by drawing simple stick figures using ovals and lines with dots for joints. Joseph stands beside Mary who is seated and holding the baby Jesus.

Add a construction line for Joseph's staff.

Add another two stick figures for the wise men at either side of the picture. Draw in the manger alongside Mary.

Draw in the third wise man kneeling beside Mary.

Sketch in the shape of the clothes, paying particular attention to the way the fabrics drape. Draw in the facial features and the wise men's footwear.

Use shading to accentuate the folds in the figures' robes and the texture of their clothing.

Add in the wise men's gifts that they are offering to the baby Jesus.

Add the wise men's boots.

Erase unwanted construction lines.

31

Glossary

Chiaroscuro The practice of drawing high contrast pictures with a lot of black and white, but not much grey.

Composition The arrangement of the parts of a picture on the drawing paper.

Construction lines Guidelines used in the early stages of a drawing. They are usually erased later.

Fixative A type of resin used to spray over a finished drawing to prevent smudging. **It should only be used by an adult.**

Light source The direction from which the light seems to come in a drawing.

Perspective A method of drawing in which near objects are shown larger than faraway objects to give an impression of depth.

Pose The position assumed by a figure.

Proportion The correct relationship of scale between each part of the drawing.

Silhouette A drawing that shows only a flat dark shape, like a shadow.

Vanishing point The place in a perspective drawing where parallel lines appear to meet.

Index

B
battling dragons 26-27
birth of a dragon 14-15

C
charcoal 6-7
Chinese dragon 11
claws 15, 19, 21, 23, 25, 27, 29, 31
construction lines 12, 26

D
dragon and slayer 28-29
dragon head 12

E
eyes 12, 15, 17, 18, 19, 28

F
fire 13, 18, 27, 30
fire and ice dragons 30-31
fire-breathing dragon 18-19
flying dragon 24-25

H
head 12, 14-26, 28-31

I
ink 6

L
light 27-29

M
mouth 12, 13, 19, 27-28, 31

P
paper 6
pastels 6-7
pencils 6-7
pens 6-7
perched dragon 22-23
perspective 8-9

R
references 10-11

S
scales 12-15, 17, 21, 25, 27, 29, 31
shade 27
silhouette 6
skin 13, 15, 17, 19, 21, 23
sleeping dragon 16-17
St George 10

T
talons 17, 21
teeth 12-13, 17, 19, 23, 29
tone 25, 31

W
wings 11, 14-15, 17, 19, 20-25, 27, 29, 31

W
Welsh dragon 10
wise dragon 20-21
Wyvern 11